Animals Change and Grow

by Bonita Ferraro

Scott Foresman
is an imprint of

Glenview, Illinois • Boston, Massachusetts • Chandler, Arizona
Upper Saddle River, New Jersey

Photographs

Every effort has been made to secure permission and provide appropriate credit for photographic material. The publisher deeply regrets any omission and pledges to correct errors called to its attention in subsequent editions.

Unless otherwise acknowledged, all photographs are the property of Pearson Education, Inc.

Photo locators denoted as follows: Top (T), Center (C), Bottom (B), Left (L), Right (R), Background (Bkgd)

Cover (CL, BC) Jupiter Images; **1** (TL, BC) Jupiter Images; **3** (TR, TL, BR, BL) Getty Images; **4** Paul Brough/Alamy Images, Rick & Nora Bowers/Alamy Images; **5** (T, C) Getty Images; **6** (C) ©Jane Burton/DK Images, (TL) ©Maximilian Weinzierl/Alamy Images; **7** (TR) DK Images, (T) Frank Greenway/DK Images, (B) Jane Burton/DK Images; **8** (TR, TL, CL, BR) Jupiter Images.

ISBN 13: 978-0-328-50759-7
ISBN 10:   0-328-50759-8

7 8 9 10 11 V010 16 15 14 13

Do you know that animals grow
and change?
A kitten and a puppy do.
Let's visit some other animals.

Look at the baby bird.
Baby birds crawl out of eggs.
Wait for time to pass.

The birds will grow and change.
They've got feathers now.
The birds will push off and fly away.

Look at the baby gerbil.
It is not done growing.
Wait for time to pass.
The gerbil will get big and grow fur.

Look at the baby tadpole.
At first, it looks like a fish.
Wait for time to pass.
The tadpole will turn into a frog.

Look at the caterpillar.
Wait for time to pass.
It is a pupa in a chrysalis.
Then it turns into a beautiful butterfly.